– The Mirabelles

The Mirabelles

Annie Freud studied English and European Literature
at the University of Warwick. Her first collection,
The Best Man That Ever Was, received the Glen Dimplex
New Writers Award. She works as a poetry tutor and
lives in Dorset with her husband.

Also by Annie Freud

The Best Man That Ever Was

Annie Freud

The Mirabelles

PICADOR POETRY

First published 2010 by Picador
an imprint of Pan Macmillan, a division of Macmillan Publishers Limited
Pan Macmillan, 20 New Wharf Road, London N1 9RR
Basingstoke and Oxford
Associated companies throughout the world
www.panmacmillan.com

ISBN 978-0-330-51907-6

'Marc Almond Poem' is based on the article 'Why did I live?',
an interview by Simon Hattenstone with Marc Almond. This
article appeared on page 12 of the Film & Music section of the
Guardian on Friday 8 June 2007.

9 8 7 6 5 4 3 2 1

A CIP catalogue record for this book is available from
the British Library.

Printed in the UK by CPI Mackays, Chatham ME5 8TD

Visit **www.picador.com** to read more about all our books
and to buy them. You will also find features, author interviews and
news of any author events, and you can sign up for e-newsletters
so that you're always first to hear about our new releases.

for Dave, May, Annabel, Eve, Rose,
Carl, Dawn and Barbara

Contents

The Wreathed Jug

The Mirabelles

Squid Sonnet

The look you shot me, milk-blue squid of Kimmeridge,
was one of recognition.
To you, I must have seemed an ogre, the kind that mothers
warn their children of. Something in you stiffened –

and the whole wild treble-clef of you leapt five foot
clear of the water,
then vanished through the bladder-wrack. Love you as I did,
I would have been the death of you.

And so, half-honoured and half-humbled,
I went back along the beach to the obsessive clink
of fossil-hunters' hammers, and the burdened buggies,

over the bridge and up the narrow, foot-worn path
where the eyes of people coming down declined
to meet the eyes of those returning to their cars.

The Mirabelles

A young poet visits an older poet
who has enjoyed fame and success.

In the street, a plum tree has scattered
its golden fruit all over the pavement.

When it's over, she'll come back and fill
her pockets with these Mirabelles.

She leaves the older poet's house;
night has fallen; she has forgotten

the plums. But the thought of them,
lying so sweet all over the pavement,

comes back to her and she remembers
them every day for the rest of her life.

Pheasant

Driving home from Winterbourne Abbas
with chipolatas, chops and cheese,
I pass a pheasant dead on the road.
I hit the brakes, put the car in reverse.
Her body is warm, her plumage intact.
I pick her up by her scaly feet
and, laying her gently in the boot,
home I go with my fabulous loot.
Working fast with criminal haste,
I pluck the feathers against the grain,
trying not to tear her skin.
I chop off her feet, her head, her wings,
knocking the knife with the rolling-pin
to make my cuts strike clean.
I open her body and pull out her guts,
her lungs, her heart and pearly eggs;
I throw them out in the unread paper,
setting aside the morsel of liver.
Her flesh is coral brushed with silver,
her fat, the colour of buttercups.

Lust

for Brian Maguire

You said you'd never been in love but that lust is wonderful,
and repeated the word several times . . . *Lust* . . . *Lust* . . .
with your eyes shining. You said it was not about the right
woman but something to do with your personality. You
asked me what being in love means; I said it was feeling
wonderful when the person you're in love with is in the
same room with you, that it has a childish aspect, and that
your heart beats faster when you think about them or say
their name, and that you feel a bit crazy and you want to
have sex all the time and keep changing your clothes and
you can't get on with your life or settle to anything, that
you want them to stop talking to other people and only
talk to you.

Then you looked at the rows of bottles and the bunches
of hops hanging from the ceiling and, spreading your
fingers along the counter, you said that if a gunman came
into the bar right now, you were prepared to lose your life
to save the lives of other people, even if you didn't know
them, or love them, or have the slightest interest in them.
And yesterday when I saw you again, you said that if any
of these other people, whose lives you'd be willing to save
from a killer, tried to kill me, you'd kill them without a
second thought.

Head of a Woman

I remember the mornings before Pap died
long before I'd heard of things like suicide,
the teacups sprigged with dark blue flowers,
your Chinese robe embroidered with towers,
peonies, dragons and battling cranes,
rubbing Windolene on the window panes,
your Beethoven hairdo, striped like a badger's,
the coat you bought me from Swan and Edgar's,
my Milky Way sliced wafer thin,
the satiny texture of your skin,
the way you said *parsley* and *sickening brute*
with the R rolled and the U drawn out,
the kisses you blew me from your fingertips,
magnificent old person, my perfectionist.

The Imitation of Derek

for Sophie

Standing on the shingle between Lydd and Dungeness
his jaunty black and yellow shack lights up the emptiness.
The power station, silver grey, like a flat for *Huis Clos*
recalls a world you've read about where flowers hardly grow,
and where each shiny clot of tar and shivered flake of rust
seems to whisper the cacophonies of atavistic lust,
and by the sea that surges, drags and grinds with allegories
of heedless ships like those shot down in shooting galleries,
a sign, hand-painted, warns the curious not to come too close:
BEWARE! These hazardous structures are in constant use.

You can't deny the magic: horehound, lad's love, clary sage,
stinging hawksbeard, viper's bugloss, poppies, saxifrage,
Quixotic pikestaffs manacled with wreaths of holey stones,
Donne's sun on the wall and driftwood capped with bones.
Distress had come to Homebase in these deadbeat weekend states
of love's remembered seasons, which the mind accumulates.
He found the one he loved the best. A good man's hard to find.
In eau-de-nil, and ten feet high, he painted FUCK ME BLIND.

The Intermediate Zone

For Lal Wickremaratne

There were home-made devils
tied to the roofs of all the village houses
and, it being November, I asked you
if this was a hangover of Guy Fawkes,
from the days of British rule.
A kind of intimacy had been established
between us, and as the astonishing figure
of the Buddha in an aureole of scallops
blotted out the sky like vast blancmange,
you tapped my knee with your forefinger
and said *Eliminate the Darkness, my friend.*

You pointed out the monkeys playing catch
on the balconies, the red-rumped bulbuls
perched on the fence-posts, and a man
with a scorpion on the flat of his spade
and I felt my phone give out in my pocket.
We drove along the wide street where women,
famed for their yellow, pink and lilac dresses,
sold fruit to the passing trade, looking for an adaptor
for my charger, and it came to me that adaptors
can only go outwards from their countries of origin,
and this was confirmed by the vendor in the shop
where electrical goods were sold.

We were feeling peckish and stopped at a stall
that sold phosphorescent garden furniture
and had a round of drinks and pale fried eggs
with peas in the echoing canteen, and watched
the giant monitor lizards sifting the garbage
while you recited Gray's Elegy and advanced
Bawa's Model of Intelligent Luxury. In the museum
a graceful young woman with impeccable diction
and a mild but educative manner showed me
the goggle-eyed Mask of Temporary Madness.
That's the one for me, I thought, and felt better
immediately.

Sting's Wife's Jam Has Done You Good

You pass me some nougat
on the point of your knife

that looks like one I used to have,
that I bought in France, that never went blunt

and was lost in the debris of a moules marinières.
Was that the bell? I hear you inquire.

No, I reply. I think it's a bird.
You are painting a restaurateur.

More nougat is cut.
What was that noise?

It's a bird in the garden
having a squawk.

The model's upstairs.
We kiss and we part.

The Case of the Egyptologist's Honey-Pot

Our topic for the evening was the Cult of Death.
It was the final session of the Summer Term.

I'd perorated on a dead man's *Ib*, his *Ba*,
his *Ren*, his *Ka*, his *Swt*, the Opening of the Mouth,

the Weighing of the Heart against the Feather
on the Scales of *Ma'at*, Anubis supervising the procedure,

Thoth recording the result and how, if all was well,
he'd be laid with all his wealth inside the *Mastaba*,

his inner organs packed into canopic jars.
The brain was never kept. He'd live again among the stars

to hunt and fish for ever in the blissful fields of *Yalu*.
I fetched the honey-pot as usual from my cabinet.

I'd had it from a cunning Argentinean
who'd made a study of the roots of human woe,

in payment for my catalogue of his collection
which was never published. It was very long ago.

It was our custom after class, to hand the pot around
and each one poked a finger in and scooped a nailful,

communing in the pleasures of the clandestine.
How fond I was of them, my bunch of amateurs,

and my favourite, the pretty Bostonian,
with her throaty vowels, always the slowest to pay me,

the way she importuned me with her questions
and with her gracile witchery, detained me.

There's something in here, she said. *I can feel it!*
and lifted out a coal-black finger, perfectly preserved.

They froze. They goggled, clapped their hands
over their mouths and shrieked: *Jesus! Christ!* and *Bloody Hell!*

I fancied it was beckoning to me, curved and wetly
glistening on her palm. It was not unlike a birth.

Poor man, she said. *I think he died another death.*
I sat there while they prattled on about a film

where neither profiteer nor scholar have the wit to read
the fatal squiggle on the map that reappears in every cloud,

in the patterns on a cobra, dozing in a haversack,
in the quicksand where a camel-boy is drowned.

Nothing can deter the adventurers' murderous lust
as full of loathing for each other, they sweat and squeeze

into the claustral fissure, skulls crumbling under boot-heels,
until a catch is sprung, a patch of loosened shale gives way,

and they're catapulted down a chute into the chamber
where the king lies buried with his treasure, bolts of linen,

and all the creatures of the Nile, in brilliant colour on the wall.
The air chills. A sharp wind blows. The torches flicker out.

A hideous mechanism grumbles into life. Pulleys whine,
columns shriek apart, platonic solids plummet from the roof,

a vast grimacing mouth snaps open, vomits
a thousand wriggling snakes and curses those that stole his joy.

And every member of that crew finds death, one in a pit
of boiling magma, another in a hail of knives, others in the bellies
of the crocodiles, the worst transfixed by his own fear.
Except for the rueful airman who's seen it all before and the girl
with a smudge across her cheek, like Mr and Mrs God and Goddess,
they head for Cairo in his battered Jeep. My stomach ached for dinner.
I put the finger back into the pot and locked the house.
There was more I could have told them: Monstrous Ammit –
part-crocodile, part-lion, part-hippopotamus – waiting by the scales
in case the heart was heavier than the feather. Heavy hearts was what he ate.
And that it was common practice, even for the burial of kings,
to switch the real heart for a surrogate.

The Yes and the No and the Terrible Thank You

I don't know what to say about you.
There is nothing to say about you,
except that you are in my mind,
hideous complexity.

It is only a film that I have watched
too many times, and I have often driven
long distances, worrying about money
and the people I have wronged.

Many films have swamps
with dead bodies hidden in them
and I feel implicated when the car
is winched to the surface.

Then everything will be proven,
the wounds and the weapon,
the approximate times of death,
the missing girls, poor Arbogast.

We are almost at the end.
I can go back to my own swamp
and its wise-cracking inhabitants,
their stitches coming loose.

The psychiatrist's theory is watertight.
She was a clinging, demanding woman.
He was always bad. The *Yes* and the *No*
and Marion, for whom no one cried
and the terrible *Thank you*.

Daube

i.m. W.G.

Towards midnight, he shouted: carrots!
and the nurse put down her cup.
– What's that, dear? Were you dreaming?
– I was not dreaming . . . I was in Paris.

There was a place I used to go
and have a dish of melting beef
that always came with *carottes Vichy*.
Is it still there? Does anyone know?

It must be possible to find someone
who knows the recipe for melting beef,
Juliette Greco sitting on my knee,
and *carottes Vichy*. How was it done?

Sunflowers

for Barbara

You complained about the sunflowers,
the way their blackened heads
all faced exactly the same way,
and that nothing else grew there.

They were sinister to me too,
but I took their part.
There were millions of them
and only one of you.

The Story of Menstruation

Today we watched a film:
The Story of Menstruation.

I lay in bed all afternoon
listening to music
with my clothes on,

thinking about the moose-head
and his frilly antlers.

Christmas Poem

for May

He went shooting,
shot a partridge,
took it round
to his girlfriend
who wasn't in
so he pushed it
through the letterbox,
hoping everything
would be all right.

The Carvery Experience

She wore a low-backed silken sweater
slung with many golden chains
that slid together when she laughed
and parted when she pulled a cracker;

and when the cracker's spark had flashed
a whistle fell into his plate;
he blew three notes into her ear
and crowned her with his paper hat.

The walls were hung with tapestries
of ladies in their courtly busks.
A boar's head was the centrepiece
with silver apples on its tusks.

I think that stag is watching us,
she said. *My tarte Tatin's gone cold.*
If we don't leave right now, I'll die.
They paid and went without a word.

Was the sweater *Dry Clean Only*?
Were the golden chains detachable?
Did the cashier say, *we've sold*
an awful lot of those this Christmas?

Monte Baldo

She handed me my peasant costume colouring book
and watched me fill the woman's bodice in with black,
her bell-shaped skirt in blue and yellow stripes,
the shepherd's jerkin and his britches in a doggy brown.
She leaned her shoulder into mine and filled the woman's
lips in red and gave the man a massive green moustache.

I saw how fine my mother's ankles were in their sheer stockings,
her supple hand-made moccasins, the bright numerals
of her small black-faced wristwatch, inhaled the lemon smell
of her cologne, revered her double rope of pearls,
her accoutrements of calf-skin, tweed and tortoiseshell –
her strike against the disappointments of her life.

I walked up to the counter. The waitress pointed to a door
that led down into the cellar, dark, wonderfully cool
and smelling of the earth, filled with boxes of tomatoes,
and a yard like the bottom of a well and at its end,
the toilet with a tiny glassless window high up on the wall.
I sat down and saw a mountain magnified against the sky.

She never told me why we stayed there for so long.
Were we hiding from something or someone?
She was the favourite with all the shopkeepers.
Every week she'd have her hair done. It was too hot
for me to leave our *pensione*. Most days she lay in bed,
looking at photos of Mastroianni and Lollobrigida.

The Inexplicable
Human Gorgeousness

The Peculiar Clucking that Indicates Regret

for Dave

Garnier, who was on better form than he was on Monday,
seemed to do with the balls as he willed.

He won the bank when Play was called at 8.18,
and made a run of 10 very graceful billiards,
leaving Ives an easy set-up – the latter accumulating 47
as his first inning, ending with a jump-shot on the long rail.

He showed how the balls may be nursed by the expert,
in spite of restrictions that are placed on the player
to curb the nursing habit.

Garnier opened the second with a block of 7 beauties,
using the draw-and-follow to the best possible advantage.
Ives followed with 9 from open-table play, the last,
a blistering massé on the upper centre of the table,
followed by a miss of an even easier massé.

In the third, Garnier put 33 to his credit,
the fourth, a three-cushion around-the-table shot,
with a very fine touch to the first object ball
and the most delicate of acute angles.

This brought the balls to the head of the table,
where all the rest of the shots were made, until a break
on the thirty-third called for a spread draw from the centre
to the right rail. This he missed by the narrowest margin.
Eighteen shots, mostly on round-table and cushion-play,
completed Garnier's fourth, to which Ives responded with a run of 56,
of which 47 were made along the baulk lines.

An easy draw, missed through carelessness or overconfidence,
put Garnier out for 8 in the next inning. On the tenth shot,
Ives got the balls together at the upper end of the table
where he petted, coaxed, cajoled, nursed and fondled them
until he had 24 to his credit. They broke out, but on the twenty-
eighth
he had them back again and, handling them as tenderly as any
lover
pats his demoiselle, held them until he had 72 to his credit.

Once more, they broke away as the result of a petulant kiss,
and he toyed with them until he had added 8 to his score.
At the lower rail he resumed his nursing tactics, the balls
responding
as if hypnotized. The ninety-first shot was a brilliant massé –
the cue ball moving less than four inches, caressing the object
balls
without moving them any perceptible distance from their resting
place.

On the ninety-seventh he had them in anchor, and when the
hundredth carom
was called by the Colonel, there was the heartiest round of
applause
heard since the cordial welcome afforded to Garnier
on his reappearance before American billiard lovers.

From the seventy-eighth to the one hundred and fourth,
there was a break to the right-hand corner,
and the balls ran back and forth in the most coquettish fashion
  – delicacy of touch,
absolute accuracy of the drives and draws for position being
the features,

until the one hundred and forty-fifth shot, when a bank shot in
    the corner
elicited the liveliest applause.

The one hundred and forty-seventh was a difficult drive,
three balls resting in a space no larger than a saucer's.
And the balls clicked lively and merry until a kiss
on the one hundred and ninety-ninth broke them,
and left both object balls against the cushion
on the lower rail, just two feet apart.

The spectators stood as one body, for it was the critical point
and meant either a score of 200 and a bad break,
or an extremely risky shot for position across the table.

A chorus of *Too Bad!* and *Hard Luck!* and the peculiar clucking
that indicates regret greeted the player.

One hundred and ninety-nine, and he'll have made the next one!
called the Colonel to the Marker. This confident remark relieved
the crowd's anxiety and seemed to determine Ives's course of
    action.
He abandoned the position idea, played for the shot
and scored his two-hundredth, the crowd applauding wildly.
It left the balls badly spread, necessitating a two-cushion shot
of great delicacy – which Ives missed.

That ended the most brilliant display of the game.

New York Times – 1 April 1896

Janine and the Somerset Liggers

They ate the muesli she made for the guests.
They broke her china and jemmied her desk.
They laddered her tights. They stirred up a crisis
and gave aggravation at the Benefits Office.
They praised her in a way that made her feel a fool.
Twice they drove the van into the dry-stone wall.
They scratched her CDs and unravelled her crochet.
Her favourite seashell was used as the ashtray.
When she drew up a rota, they laughed till they cried
then forgot to feed the dog and it almost died.
When at last she protested they said they'd rather
leave this dump and go back to their father
than listen to any more nagging and bitching –
a terrible silence fell in the kitchen.
They sat there and watched while she gouged from the split
in the length of the table some pieces of grit,
some currants and peas, miscellaneous crumbs
which she swept in a heap between fingers and thumbs
and bludgeoned to dust with the back of her spoon,
then she lay down and wailed like a wolf at the moon.
So they calmed her down with a heavenly bong
and took her to bed where they pleasured her long.

Brandenburg

– What kind of psychotherapy do you practise?
– It is called Terralussologie.
– I have never heard of it.
– No one has. Here is my brochure.

Earth: *terra*. Moon: *lus*. Sun: *sol*.
Everyone is born on the earth, the basis for all.
Some people are born on a sunny day.
They live more on the outside.

Their arms are raised; they look at the sky.
Others are born at night, when the sky is dark.
They are more interior and live in their minds;
they cross their arms, like you.

– Is it a talking therapy or is it psychodynamic?
– Neither. I work with breath.
Some people breathe deeply;
others breathe little and short,

high up in the neck, a sort of puffing.
These people can be a bit lacking in life.
There are few people in Brandenburg
and they know nothing of psychotherapy.

They think it is stupid; some are Nazis.
They try to make some tourism
but they don't have the right attitude.
This is the old East Germany.

Spleen on Berwick Street

Again, Howard Jacobson's got there before me.
He's there on the lilac banquette;
He's eating a cake in the shape of a rose
with a girl in a lampshade hat.

Later on, he will have to go home
and write about panic and style;
His daughter will tackle a sonorous fugue
and then he'll lie down for a while.

His wife will come in and he'll run her a bath
and help her step out of her dress;
he'll bring her a drink and make her forget
all the things that she cannot express.

He'll be tempted to mention the old cabbage leaves
that squelched underfoot and whose smell
gave a lift to his mood; a squeeze from her hand
says she loves him and all's going well.

The Breast-Fed and the Un-Breast-Fed

i.m. W.M.

     – I can't go on like this. I who look out on the world and
  retreat in horror.
With your perfect marriage, you make me feel I'm fit for nothing
       but houses, meals and curtain fabric.

     The way you have of not caring if your flights are cancelled
(It would be a total disaster for *us!*) and just walk up to the desk
       and book a holiday to somewhere else.

     Your work for the rehabilitation of violent offenders
on top of all you have achieved in industrial relations
       and literacy, and now the *Incorruptible Elbow Joint*,

     your latest pioneering invention, make me feel
I'm going mad. All our lives, ever since we got here in 1933
       as children, you were my protector, helped me to feel British,

     found me this house, befriended both my husbands
one after the other, took the children sailing on the Broads
       in summer, but I don't know if I can see you any more.

                   *

     – Please don't do this. I am not, and have never been,
terribly intuitive and may often seem blunt and self-absorbed.
     If you really knew me, perhaps you'd realise

that my life has been less satisfying than it appeared,
and nothing much can be gained by these comparisons
	although I understand why you do it

	and really sympathise. I, being the first-born, breast-fed one,
had the advantage. And I'd so hate it if you did this
	because I'd spend the rest of my life concocting schemes

	to get you back. I'll do absolutely anything you ask
not to lose you, except put up with the horrible thought
	of you endlessly putting up with me.

Marc Almond Poem

I couldn't talk properly after the accident.
I still have periods of mental confusion
and can't memorise things very well
and I have problems with my speech,
though it's getting better now.

You're meant to have this feeling of hooray,
I'm alive, and I should be grateful
but I thought, why did I live?
Why couldn't it have just finished for me
then I wouldn't have to go through all this.
What am I going to do – just have all these years
of not being able to sing again?

Sometimes I feel I've got to run away
and I did many times feel like that.
I thought: people are going to laugh at me,
they're going to see me forgetting things.
They're going to see me not being able
to stand up properly. I feel
I'm going to be a freak show.

I was hyperventilating, I was feeling sick,
it was a big heavy cloud hanging over my life.
I walked out on stage for the first time in three years
and the microphones didn't work,
and everything was going wrong technically
and I thought, do I run off stage screaming,
have a tantrum, shout at the sound-guy
or just look like an idiot?

But I put down the microphone,
walked out into the audience and sang the song
and that broke the spell of stage fright.
I thought: I'd rather be on stage than anything.
That's the only time I feel fulfilled
and that I'm alive.

Cod's Roe for a Crying Woman

for Irmgard Osterberger and Tim Wells

Don't cry, you'll make your make-up run.
How much have you had to drink?

The occasion requires some grand gesture,
but what? You can't stay here, boozing.

On your feet. Take my arm. Where can we go?
Perhaps you're cold. Perhaps you'd like a hat.

Look at this one with the green feathers,
ideal for a walk in the mountains.

Close your bag. There are thieves about.
Perhaps you're hungry. Hah! *Eingebung*!

Here is a fish shop. It looks so inviting.
Fishmonger! I'll take that piece of cod's roe.

A drop of vinegar, for the lady. Isn't that nice?
Now let's go to the Park and watch the nannies

walking to and fro with babies in their prams.
Look at these tulips. What a lovely yellow!

These trees must be hundreds of years old.
Here is a good bench. Sit down. Next to me.

Dry your face on my handkerchief. It's clean,
a gift from my mother. Now it's lunchtime.

Open wide . . . wider. That's a good girl.
What a story to tell your grandchildren.

Just to prove I'm no monster, I'm having some too.
Quite tasty. Another piece? You've had enough?

You remind me of someone. Here comes the rain.
Here's a cab. Quick, before we both get soaked.

Big Top

A horse rears above
in the dome of navy blue
and with fingers and with eyes
I appeal to the rider
restrain your animal
but it's him and he knows
me inside out
and I cannot say the words
or move my arm away
from the loose purple lips
and the yellow teeth
and the pain will be terrible
and all I am or ever was
is the prospect of being bitten
in public by a horse

Naked Child Laughing

The light, mind you, is strong and uniform;
nothing is lost in shadow; there is no rhetoric of mystification;
broad strokes articulate the forearm, wrist and knuckle
with a freedom that suggests
the excitement of a deep engagement.

A long thin swipe of white gets over the girl's gleaming,
bony shin, while thick zigzags of brown convey
the hair falling around her hand.

Do we need to know why the child is laughing?
Or indeed that she is the artist's daughter?
Not in the least.

What matters is that we register her presence
with the greatest possible immediacy:
the inexplicable human gorgeousness.

— Sebastian Smee, from 'Lucian Freud'

Strawberry Festival

Just a little drive, they promise. It's all of eighty miles
through towns where the price of houses have fallen;
no one wants to live there but the gay and very poor
and Rock City Relics sells diamanté frog-pins, rag-time
biscuit tins and bell-hop uniforms from the defunct hotels.
The Hudson flashes between the trees and I remember a film
where a man weeps on a Greyhound bus for the man he could
    have been.
I see the flattened faces of a hundred dead raccoons.
A screen door bangs in the wind and a girl leafs a magazine.

We come to a green valley and a great field with a marquee
and a climbing frame for the kids topped with hawk-heads.
Women in long cotton gowns, with grey plaits down their backs,
serve strawberries at the trestles, pass the jugs of cream,
hold out long fingers, saying: *I am Dorothy, I'm Cordelia.*
Welcome to our Strawberry Festival. You're from England, right?
Soft-footed futures-analysts and professors of French Literature
in wide-awakes and button-downs, sip from the lip of a ladle.
Gary's talking alimony: *she's killin' me man, even with my tenure!*

We eat our fill, we take our seats and one gets up with his wife –
she was with the Weathermen, now she's with the Peace Corps –
takes his Gibson from its case and sings us songs of the brothers
fallen in the fight for pay, for schools, lungs full of corn dust,
devouring Whitman, Dickinson, Poe – whatever came *their* way –
the bark of the boss's dog, the crack of his henchman's whip,
their starving children, their copperplate, and rickets,
hands raw from gleaning grain, huddled under sacks,
six in a bed and keep your daughter pure for her wedding day.

And the women sing close harmony of a double yoke of pain,
stitching in lamp-light, selling their hair, those cakes that melted
in your mouth, looting coals, the struggle for the big idea –
Diphtheria! Eviction! Pop's DTs! Stay-for-Church-Fricassee!
of a summer gown for courting days, cut down for little sisters,
worn till the flower print had gone and cut again for granny rags,
shame-on-you-for-speakin-so-you-no-bigger'n-a-who-ore's-cra-ab,
of the sons shot full of holes for nothing on the fields of France,
sorrel sprouting from eye-sockets: Robbie. Phil. Elmer. Frank.

Maidenhair

They landed on the beach just before noon
and immediately he found a spray of maidenhair,
fossilized on slate, lying in a rock pool.
Out of habit, he looked around for more
but found nothing, at least nothing for him.
There were pebbles of a most sensuous white
and pieces of green glass roughened by the tides
that, as a younger man, he would have kept;
but he no longer had a desire for such things.

The skipper and his mate were scraping the scales
off the fish they'd caught, and began frying them
over a fire of tangled roots and grass.
The shingle was splitting and singing in the embers
and a delicious smell rose from the pan.
Saliva filled his mouth in an unwonted gush.
They sat and ate the hot sticky flakes and crisped skin
and the beer bottle passed from hand to hand.

The sun was hotter now and his trousers felt tight
and while the men busied themselves with the boat
he went and stretched out in a sandy hollow
between the tamarisks that grew close to the shore,
mobbed with hundreds of chirruping finches.
He pulled the slate from the pocket of his jacket
and lay in the posture of a girl in a painting
he'd seen the day before, naked on a bed,
staring in a mirror, encircled with pearls.

Identical Fugitive Octopus

He drove to the edge of the city and parked the Subaru
in a long street he remembered from previous visits.

Nothing had changed. The small shop that sold
lace collars and haberdashery was still there

and the hand-written price labels were exactly
as he remembered them, even the way the ink had faded.

The church bell sounded four o'clock and suddenly the air
was full of the smell of biscuits, over the warm stink of drains.

A minute, scrofulous cat had followed him down
to the front, past the restaurants offering fasolakia

and kleftiko, depicted in colour under greying plastic,
and waited in hope on the corner while he trailed

round the stalls festooned with copies of the Evzones' dress,
the stiff skirts, white stockings and pom-pommed shoes,

the eye, hand and foot of Michelangelo's David,
the Colossus of Rhodes with his upturned prick,

rows of nereids, their hair half-hiding their small breasts,
sitting cross-legged on scallop shells, dinner plates

with curly-bearded Poseidon waving his trident
at the passing ships, and vases in every imaginable size

painted with the identical fugitive octopus,
and shelves of resin globes enclosing underwater scenes

of coral, shells and seaweed, treasure from wrecks.
He bought a bottle of Metaxa and a bag of macadamias

a porno magazine and a pack of Lucky Strikes
and climbed the steps to his rented room

overlooking the harbour and lay on the bed, eating
and drinking, looking at the pictures that hung on the wall:

the dolphin frescoes from the Palace of Knossos
and the snow-capped peaks of the White Mountains.

Thunder in the Middle of the Lake

for Patric

Live at peace with yourself;   that is the high dream,
that's what Dante meant. You may feel it's complacent, even egotistical,
always to write about yourself, and the irksome ebbing of your illusions.

But if you take all that away   what do you have left?
Don't go for shoddy things.   Let love be your master.
The high dream goes on being indispensable. Especially in these times.

Gagging for the Canon

The militia stops for sandwiches.
The outlook seems uncertain.
An ambush would be welcome.
I check the mail to see what gives.
       The beautiful flints in the river
       are the beautiful flints in the river.
       I hope for a change in the weather.
       I'm gagging for the canon.

I speak into the trumpet
of your freeze-dried daffodil.
The more I scrape the barrel
the hollower it rings.
       Beware of illustrious birds,
       be they black or be they white.
       They're the ones that shoot you down.
       I'm gagging for   the canon.

My thoughts are like rutting Chihuahuas.
My tropes like rendered marrow.
I'm like an old geranium-filled
wheelbarrow in the snow.
       Once there were wild horses.
       They're on the other side of the river.
       The drums are getting fainter.
       I'm gagging for   the canon.

The Wreathed Jug

The poems which follow derive from letters and
conversations with my mother, Kitty Garman,
over the last twenty years.

Marrying Strange Men

I cannot dodge you, though I have tried
to dodge the fact of your insistence that all
anemones be Japanese, that your hand-milk's smell
is redolent of almonds, your allergy to bees,

your wayward toothpicks in their livid green,
your migraines, your eyebrows plucked to non-existence,
your beauty, your invention of the disease
that only those with stripy irises contract,

your love of Proust, your hatred of machines,
your letters from the US full of deprecation
of their Groundhog Day, full of longing for English
laissez-faire, of illustrations of your CAT scans,

venal chiropractors, contemplations on a glass
of Pinot Grigio, the walnut shade of Cowper's Tiney,
the acquisition of a bouclé jacket, the prowler in the topiary,
your fear of Hell, your envy of rich women.

The book you meant to write about your life
would have been called *Marrying Strange Men*.

O, These Men, These Men

Cloyed and sickened by Colette's crude rusticities –
too many teats & nipples, too much self-praise –
I turned to Shakespeare last night – the heartbreaking scene
in *Othello*, where Desdemona is having a goodnight talk
with her worldly-wise companion. She sings her song
about the Willow and the Forsaken Maid, and she bursts out:
O, these men, these men. I felt it was the cry of all women
all over the world in their mystification at this other sex
who behave so inexplicably, yet somehow are so necessary,
unwieldy as they may be.

Emilia's response is so sensible & comforting –
& reminds her mistress that women can be as lustful,
fickle & perverse, & that perhaps it may all be a game.

Was in floods myself & went to bed,
having made myself a rather nasty omelette,
eggs being the only provender in the house.

Ute

I will try to tell you about Ute; she is so complex; it is quite difficult.
She sails into the gym, swathed in scarves; red hat pulled down low,
gauntlets, olive skin, Burmese-cat blue eyes behind dark glasses,
thigh-booted, and with great swooping laughs and greetings.
Her car is sporty, and in winter has pale grey furry covers,
not only on the seats, but on the steering wheel and safety belts.

It's crammed with baskets of food, jars of honey, eggs and flowers.
She always carries a fringed, hammocky bed that doubles
as her yoga mat; the whole effect has a swingy, gypsy elegance.
In action she is very good and lithe. She was once a modern dancer,
then turned to teaching yoga. She is exactly the same age
as I am, is of German origin, and has been married twice.

When the war broke out she was on holiday in the Baltic
on the family yacht. She was sent to Pomerania to avoid the bombs.
After the war, her family, military aristos, disgusted at the upstart Hitler,
moved to Hungary to start again. Her father and brother committed suicide,
the Russians invaded Hungary, and with husband, son and mother
she came to America to live down the shame and horror of it all.

She claims she knew all about the concentration camps
and the Holocaust when she was only 13. She detests social life
and never goes to parties. She prefers the company of cats,
young addicts, and devotes herself to her bed-ridden mother of 98
who does not speak a word of English. She's vestigially Catholic,
permanently Buddhist and is full of love, laughter and givingness.

"Ecce Homo"

Unlike you as a child, I was never overly
impressed by Daddy; there he always was,
in the studio, a great grumpy *obelisk*
of pain and endurance, & that was that,
until he was removed
to the cemetery at Putney Vale.
I neither sympathised with
nor was I frightened of him.

You may remember the car crash:
3 young boys killed (all local)
& the 4th now critically ill.
Whole village in mourning.

I heard the Priest say that prayers
for the parents and relatives of these boys
would be said in the chapel,
so I went along.

Imagine my embarrassment & annoyance
to find several mildly officious women,
re-arranging the pews into a circle
for a discussion on *the Nature of God
& what He meant to us*.

I have always fought shy
of religious discussion, but felt entrapped,
& as it would have looked rude to leave,
I stayed.

It was made very clear
that it was *not* to be a discussion,
or in any way contentious, very civilized,
but rather limiting. We were 10 women,
all (but one young girl) of about my age,
& one man, very brusque and definite.

We were all very shy, except for him;
but one by one we came out
and spoke. Lots of silences.
We had an arbiter or leader,
but she was very good & reticent.

Anyway, after some time,
we were given bits of paper
& asked to do something called "The Window Test".
One had to divide the paper
with a pencil (these were handed round)
into 4 panes:

1. God as we were taught when young,
or had thought, when young,
what he was like. I tried this eagerly.

2. God as we imagined him now.
I drew a symbol of the grail;
It looked like a teacup
in a halo of steam.

3. God as we would like him to be.

4. I have forgotten.

Most of us declined,
Saying we could not draw etc.
More contemplation, one or two silent prayers
& we left.

When I got home I looked at my drawing
& saw to my absolute amazement
that I had drawn "Ecce Homo"; down-turned mouth,
pressed-down crown of thorns, the roped hands,
the look of hard-won endurance.

All this was done absolutely unconsciously.
I had added some tears coursing down his cheeks
& then two days later to hear you talking on the video
so emphatically on the same subject!

'There are more things in Heaven & Earth, Horatio.'

The Actual Pronunciations

We have a long and beautiful drive to Massachusetts
on the Taconic Parkway – from a Red Indian word
meaning 'of the country'. No lorries or services,
just some viewing places to stare at lakes and swamps.

The road is lined with towering black rocks
where water had dripped and frozen in the night
and made a frieze of gigantic icicles. Fuzzy skeins
of sphagnum moss brush against the bonnet.

We arrive around 4 and are met by Serena
at a little diner and thence to their most
romantic farmhouse set in a grove of twisty oaks
on the site of an ancient Nipmuck settlement.

The house is made of chocolate-painted boards,
is L-shaped and trees press against the windows.
Inside all is dark and womby with 5 enormous
stone and brick fireplaces, both up and downstairs.

It's luxurious and shabby at the same time
and filled with books, shells, paintings and cats
(5, including a wild-cat tabby kitten called Fractal).
What's just so lovely is there's *too much* room,

two very large, unnecessary halls in the middle.
They each have two studies and there is a central
kitchen, 2 staircases, 2 bathrooms and many tiny
panelled cupboards with trompe-l'œil scrolls,

a stately dining room, an elegant sitting room.
Every time you open a cupboard, a new cat
jumps out, and the wild kitten has to be kept
separate from the others because they are jealous.

She will adapt, or they will. We brought them
sloe gin, a painting of red tulips that had been
waiting 4 years for Serena, and a thick silk
and wool red-and-gold scarf for Lois.

Serena hung my picture up at once;
It looked as though it had always been there.
I was pleased because I had grown unsure
of its merits as I had done it so long ago.

It was dinner time and 3 friends arrived,
one of whom had fought in the Vietnam War,
and had been wounded, physically and morally,
though by now was clearly on the mend.

Lois had been up since 1am, making salmon
mousse, cranberry sauce, gravy, stuffing,
mashed squash and a special Lebanese
garlicky salad, a 20lb turkey, pumpkin, apple

and cinnamon pies and was very sprightly
and espiègle. She's an insomniac but needs
very little sleep and so the 1am business
was all in a day's work to her.

We had lashings of wine, white and red,
and some people had whiskey. Serena,
who is empress-like and stately, never cooks
but does the wine-opening and pouring

and stacks the dishwasher. It seems to work.
(The arrangement as well as the dishwasher.)
There was no room to be shy. Our welcome
was so warm, and there were lots of jokes,

reminiscences, and some confidences.
Lois and Serena wanted to know all
about you and we showed them photos
and they were truly interested.

We went to bed, not too late, in our nooky
bedroom with black sheets and Virginia Woolf
first editions, and best of all, a kind of bird-
feeding contraption, with a two-way mirror,

so that one was awakened by a gentle tap
and saw oneself face to face with a blue jay
or long-tailed tittlemouse, through the slats
of a Japanese blind. It's difficult to describe,

and impossible to draw. By day, it looked just like
an ordinary window box. I couldn't make out
how it worked, but it gave the birds
the illusion that no one was watching them.

Next day, we drove to Boston to look
at the Art Gallery, which was modern
and enormous – crowded as it was a holiday,
but vast enough to be able to see.

There were many Matisses, early ones, luscious
Fantin-Latours, Degas's *Petits Rats* and best of all
glowing Gaugins, which I had seen all my life
in reproduction but never in the painted flesh.

They had that very large one called
Where do we come from? Who are we?
Where are we going? Very splendid
and a carved bas-relief: *Soyez amoureuses,*

vous serez hereuses. (Alas, not <u>always</u> true)
and best of all one I'd never heard of:
a naked woman, very white, lying *along* a horse,
with some other women draped in cloth,

standing round in a trance, mountains beyond,
like the best kind of dream. After this, I wanted
to go home and ponder, but it was *on* to a Japanese
Zen garden and endless shopping amid crowds.

In a bookshop, where we kept losing and finding
and losing each other, I bought Serena Ishiguro's
Artist of the Floating World and some Conté pencils
for myself, only 2 as they were expensive.

Then on to a computer shop where S and I
became restive while L and W played on the keys
and compared notes. We finally tore them away
and headed back to Auburn and the pussy-cats.

Cocktails, chicken, fresh fettuccini and early to bed
as a trip to the ocean was planned for the morrow.
W had bought an album of Beatles songs and we
nostalgically sang them to their out-of-tune piano.

More jokes, lots of good letting-down-hair talk,
nothing malicious. I must sound starved of company,
but am so used to being so, I only notice it when
I am not; being so unsocial, I only really like

it when I'm with people I am truly fond of
and who speak the same language, I don't
mean 'English', I mean are *simpatico*,
as I'm sure you know full well.

By the way, I am learning to speak 'American';
one has to, not just the words and expressions,
but the actual pronunciations. I can now say
'stamps' in the P.O. and get what I want, not just

a puzzled stare: open mouth wide, take deep
breath and say 'stare-amps', or 'stair-amps'.
Try it. No 'steer-amps' is better. I have perfected
it and do it nearly every day.

Day 3. Up early, bundle into every woolly vestment,
boots, spare boots, gloves, woolly hats, cameras,
binocs, buckets for beach specimens, and off we go
through the country, past nut-coloured houses

round village greens, white clapboard churches,
Christmas decorations, holly wreaths and Christmas
trees, then into wilder, farther country and we come
to the Atlantic – white sand, black rocks, lowering sky.

L and S look aghast! There has been a hurricane
and their favourite beach has been swept away,
rocks hurled about, roads closed, houses near
the sea shattered to pieces, their roofs blown off.

We find a way down and walk with difficulty
as the wind is strong, the tide luckily going out.
There is an island alive with breeding cormorants.
The dune called Garnet Sand. A kind of mauvy pink.

The light changes; the rocks turn green. Olivine.
It's very bracing after so much luxury
and I'm quite pleased when it begins to rain
and we can return to the comfort of the car.

I've foolishly let on that we've both had birthdays
and L has decided on a birthday lunch. We sit
in the glass-encased terrace of a seafood restaurant
overlooking a winding river which might be the Blyth

amid banks of sedgy grasses. We admire the egrets
and the nesting swans. Then suddenly *martinis* appear!
Then *Moët*! Then *freshly broiled little lobsters*!
This time I am up to it, but only just.

As we eat and drink, the river fills up, the sun sinks.
Back in the car to a nature reserve on a spit
of land called Plum Island, because of the wild
plum trees that grow so plentifully there.

We are told to look out for snowy owls but see none
just masses of migrating ducks and geese. The colours
are unbearably beautiful. The wind drops, and we
get out and photograph the sunset and each other.

Then back to the pussies, tea, drinks and turkey
sandwiches, Beatles, bed. Next day, I am very stiff
and am given a soothing herbal bath. We pack
regretfully and leave. But not before one more thing:

Lois had long felt stifled by the pecking order
of academic life and was tired of Romance Literature,
Arthurian and Icelandic myth, the Golden Bough –
she suddenly wanted a change from the admin.

Quite by chance, or by fluke, she heard that the local
Natural History Museum wanted a curator.
She applied and got the job, knowing very little
of what it entailed. Now she has total

responsibility for this lovely museum in a park
and for all the animals, alive and stuffed, the staff,
the vets, the arrangement of exhibitions, the satellite
pictures of the ocean bed, the Observatory,

the health and safety of the pythons, the owls,
chinchillas, racoons, opossums and bears.
The animals are there because they've been wounded
and are nursed back to health before their release.

She has done away with the mangy old cases
of sad, stuffed things and created living pools
filled with clams, fish, seaweed and barnacles.
All very impressive, except that I worry

about the animals that are kept in solitude.
She drove us to the turnpike, put us
on the right road and we were home
in a twinkling, dazed by so much pleasure.

The Last Ballet

The last ballet, which I had been somewhat dreading
as it was called Fearful Symmetries, and thought
it would be trying to convey eternal Blakean themes
with much heavy miming and sinewy writhing
on the floor, was a total thrill from start to finish.

It was just dancing, pure dancing, perpetual movement,
never stopping, never lapsing, just energy, light and colour.
The men were marvellous, throwing themselves
across the stage, leaping like panthers, swooping like hawks
and at times seemed almost arrested in mid-flight.

The girls were more fragile, their technique exquisite,
but never look-at-me, never descending into acrobatics.
Each pas-de-deux was erotic beyond words,
a total seduction, not in the usual balletic sense
but more in the feeling of the movement.

They danced as though it was what they *had* to do,
oblivious to the audience. The music was strange,
throbbing, harsh, percussive, almost guttural,
rising and falling, then slowing down and very quietly
they slowed down, and then *folded* down.

Acknowledgements

Some of these poems have appeared in *The London Magazine*, *The Poetry Paper*, *Notes from the Underground*, *Rising* and *Identity Parade: New British and Irish Poets* (Bloodaxe, 2010) ed. Roddy Lumsden.

'The Yes and the No and the Terrible Thank You' was commissioned for Psycho Poetica, an event conceived by Simon Barraclough to celebrate the fiftieth anniversary of Hitchcock's *Psycho*.

Naked Child Laughing is an extract from *Lucian Freud* by Sebastian Smee (Taschen Books), used with the author's permission.

Every effort has been made to contact other copyright holders of material reproduced in this book. If any have been inadvertently overlooked, the publishers will be pleased to make restitution at the earliest opportunity.

I wish to thank Alan Buckley and Sue Grindley for their thought-ful comments and advice and Don Paterson for his continued encouragement and suggestions for the manuscript.

Inside cover: *Wreathed Jug in Autumn* by Kitty Garman.